Every Stranger
Deserves
A
Poem.

Alyea S. Pierce

D1564933

Acclaim for Alyea Pierce's
Every Stranger *Deserves* A Poem

"WOW!!! Alyea Pierce speaks directly to your heart. Her creative voice is loud and clear on every page. She touches your soul and inspires you to open your hearts and minds. Keep Reading!!! Her poetic journey is a true inspiration for all, young and old. A great gift for someone you love."

> -Sonia M. Beatty, President & CEO, Targeted Business Solutions Inc. Empowering Individuals, Teams & Organizations to Achieve Greater Success

"Alyea has a way with words that makes it feel like they have jumped off the page and are carrying you to a destination she calls love. Her poetry is a reflection of so many facets and journeys in life- it's like politely being reminded of how blessed we are to feel emotions. She expresses the complexity of 'otherness' in a way that beautifully reframes it as an 'opportunity'. Her words make the reader feel at ease about not having answers always, to take risks, and to open oneself to another. You can tell that she has a deep appreciation for life, the spoken and written word, and truth. Each word and poem builds upon the other, leaving the ready ready for more. She is truly a wordsmith of the next generation."

> - Dawn J. Fraser
> Humorist, Storyteller & National Speaker

"...Once I began reading *Every Stranger Deserves a Poem*, I couldn't stop; I was completely intrigued...I am amazed by the honesty, depth, power, and clarity of Alyea S. Pierce's poetic voice."
>   -Rachel Renee Smith
>   Author of *The Rain Won't Hide These Tears*

"Alyea S. Pierce is a force of nature. A new and powerful young voice; Alyea is putting her stamp on the world of poetry and prose, with her first work; *Every Stranger Deserves a Poem. Every Stranger* is a testament to what we face the most in life, Love, Loss and how the yin and yang of their relationship forge bonds beyond measure. Alyea's Prose strips to the bone the very meanings of the most powerful force on earth, while at the same time making it profoundly human; flawed, an enigma, and beautiful. It is clear even in her young life she has experienced the wisdom of the ancestors with her moving words that take the most complex and divine thoughts, and bring them to simple and subtle truth. Profound, provocative and sincere, this collection of work goes to the very heart of all of us, lives there; makes a home. Every Stranger deserves *these poems.*"
>   -Mikal Amin Lee
>   Emcee/Founder-Fresh Roots Music
>   Program Director, Urban Word NYC

"...The character Word Smith is **you.** It felt like his words were in motion, it brought life to his characters. It left me wanting more. He also taught us how to dream..."

-James G. Hunter
Co-Founder - New Jersey Orators

"Alyea Pierce strums the strings of life, love and loss as if the heart was a musical instrument whose sounds could make strangers, fast friends. Her concept is bold, her heart is bare and the sound of the words you read is clear…"

-Toya Beasley
Media Personality
Founder & CEO of Sistafriendz

"In Alyea Pierce's first collection *Every Stranger Deserves a Poem*, her vibrant voice is apparent as she poetically reckons with themes of love and loss. She demonstrates a creative astuteness and an insightful vulnerability in "Ramen Noodles" as she wrestles with her brother's perception of black standards of beauty. As her gaze turns outward to the collective in her public poem, "Our Deepest Craving" she speaks with the urgency of a clarion call. In this collection, Pierce is busy doing the work of an emerging poet by exhibiting both tenderness and defiance by naming her truth. She is social justice fist flowering reaching out to the world."

- Glenis Redmond
Poet

Dedicated To My Aunty Sylvia.

She Always Did it Her Way

Contents.

Part III

Part IV

Go → the last section of this book to

1. Learn how to Bring
    EXCITING,
    CUSTOM-MADE
    Programs and Workshops to YOUR High
    School, University, or Community
    Organization!!!

2. Receive a DISCOUNT to the very
    FIRST Write to Speak Open Mic!

3. Tell Alyea which Poem is YOUR
    favorite and Share your very own
    work!

Is Poetry a Universal Language?

You have the Write to be Free.
-Alyea Pierce

Every Stranger Deserves A Poem is not for me. It is dedicated to all who have inspired. It is dedicated to the Lovers, Believers, Hopeful Romantics, Book worms, Loners, Awkward people, People who don't need a home to be at Home, the Folks on Wall Street, the College Dropouts, and College Graduates. This is for everyone who has felt lost or at a loss. It is for every person who has fallen out of love or stood by it. These short stories and poems are for every stranger who has lived more than what I know as living. It is for the people who wear age proudly and live wisdom. This is not for me. This is for us. No matter where you are right now, we are more in common than you think. This book is for all the strangers craving to be connected and I am merely the first person to open their heart in this conversation.

I have Loved. My, have I loved...
I have Lost and been Lost. I have asked the stars, "Why" and cursed the air too many times.
And I have Lived...and I am still living.

Thank you for taking the time to travel on **Word Smith's** journey of his most adventurous day. Word shows us that when Life, Love and Loss are all in harmony, words can combine to create Poetry. The words we speak are not *just* words. They have meaning. The *words* you use are not by mistake. They are intentional.

Poetry is the heart and You have a choice.

So, here we go. **The Challenge.** This book revolves around the idea that each of us are strangers craving to feel again, or who don't want to let go of all of the great things we feel. The world desires to be connected. So, let us get connected. The title of this book is *Every Stranger* Deserves *a Poem*, so I would love if you would join ***The Every Stranger Journey!*** Write a poem for a stranger, short or long in length, circular or square in shape, one word or a hundred for anybody or an imaginary somebody. Challenge yourself.

I have a YouTube channel, and I would LOVE if you sent your amazing poems, or feelings of this book to the YouTube channel ***The Every Stranger Journey!*** and if you have more poems, keep sending! I will repost every single one. Send videos of what you think the definition of Love, Life, and Loss are to you. Send videos of what poetry or spoken word mean to you. Spread the Word. This is a HOME for OUR art.

And who knows, if we both work earnestly and intently, there's a good chance we'll end up sitting side by side autographing books someday!

I want to thank each and every one of you for sharing your life with me and sharing your time with me. Thank you for not looking at who I am or who I am not. I appreciate you giving Life. Love. And Loss a chance.

Part I

The City.

Hello.

What a wondrous day to finally meet you.

My name is Word Smith, but you can call me Word.

I like to think of myself as a wordinary stranger living in a strange, wordy part of the world that has 13 hours in each day.

It's busy here.

Not many trees; just a lot of concrete everywhere.

Most of all though, plenty of lights that never turn off. A lot of city-like lights that would rather intrude on the night than wait for morning.

There are a lot of strangers in this area, 1,585,873, to be exact. Every 1,585,873rd stranger works for the Government, also known as Nihil. Every stranger does what they have to do to survive, not what they love and want to do. The Nihil likes it that way. All of us work in our own individual cubicles, alone, and separate. We have come to understand that it is so easy to feel alone, when you are made to believe you are. The Nihil encourages strangers to have their own space because conversation can create a connection, and connections can mean change.

There is a birth of a new stranger every 4.4 minutes and a death of a familiar one every 9.1 minutes. Everyone here, in this city, is a stranger who has a pocket full of unsaid poems—things that strangers desire to say to feel connected, and crave to feel in order to be called human again—but instead, hold their tongue. These poems that fill our pockets are the written notes grade-school children pass under

4

desks in classrooms, poems mocking Shakespeare's Sonnet 18, poems that float inside the mind and outside the mind on backs of seventh grade notebooks, and poems written for the lovers that strangers are too scared to let all of themselves love.

But, at the end of this 13-hour day, each and every one of us are craving to be connected to someone. Someone that will listen, and not speak. Someone who will speak just enough when the time is right, and make our hearts half full again. Someone who can help us feel alive. There are certain strangers in this city that want something close and want something that can leave the feeling of another stranger on their skin. However, others don't want to be held. No hugs, or anything that holds onto love longer than a stranger said they would. And then there is me. I am the kind of stranger who wants a "good" conversation, even though the word "good" is subjective. I want to listen to how our lives intertwine. This city is cold, and heartless, and I crave something that can string our hearts together.

I have noticed over break room coffee, for 10-minute intervals every three hours and simply living day to day, that there are heartstrings that connect each and every stranger in this city. No matter where a stranger comes from, no matter what language they speak, no matter their racial or economic difference, these heartstrings can connect all of us, all of humanity. So, this book is my little secret (shhhhhh), it is my unsaid poem in the back of my pocket, my story of the most exciting day of my life. The day I met the three heartstrings that connect every stranger.

Life.
Love.
and Loss.

I hope you enjoy.

Life.

**We are forever-changing humans; our needs are
always changing. When one need is filled, the next
need now has room to scream a little louder. Once
we stop changing, and living …
we begin dying.
- Alyea Pierce**

I met Life on her death bed.

      The nurses split room 727 in half. My great-
aunt received one side of the room, and Life had the
other. The room was separated by one long, white
curtain that was so flimsy and weak, they both could
hear each other's painful moans every night. Life
stayed on the side closest to the window, because my
great aunt told the nurses to put her there. Life was a
complete stranger to her, yet my great-aunt said that
looking at the nature always helped her when she was
finished with chemo for the day. Life only had one
visitor, and when my great-aunt was napping, I
enjoyed talking to Life about who she "was" (she
preferred to use past tense for some reason).

      Life was 5'4" with short brown hair and wore a
pink ribbon over her left breast every day. She had
been fighting breast cancer for over a year, and was
beginning to have hope again. As each strand of hair
grew stronger on her head, the more she had living
proof that her insides were getting stronger as well.
However, that was a false calculation.

The doctors told Life that she had a little over one

month to live.

Life used to be a wild woman. Now when I say wild, I do not mean wild like an animal, but a strong wild. She would not take no for an answer. She was a sassy kind of wild, the kind of wild that would somehow trick me into saying yes, and I would actually think I did. She was a 22-year-old woman going through 18-year-old girl phases like dying her hair, sneaking out of her own apartment (yes, the apartment she owned with her best friend) and playing in rock bands. Wild like calling out of work to sing in train stations and on stoops, and curbs built of concrete. Wild like couch-surfing and backpacking across the country.

She enjoyed the little things in life, like picking fresh fruit from trees, living with just one bag of luggage, and rolling around with her pit bull. Many strangers said she was crazy, that she was unfocused and confused, but Life was tired of having direction. She knew that she was not just running away from her problems, because she had a destination at the end of the road, even if no one else could see it.

Life was supposed to be a doctor, or at least that was what she was $60,000 in debt for. Her parents dreamed up the perfect life for her, the perfect man, the perfect job, and they knew she would be happy if she simply followed their steps to perfection. She had been following their plan of success since the day she was born. ... She was tired of living the life her parents were not able to. So, the day after graduation from college, she looked her parents in the eyes and said, "I can't do this anymore. I am tired, I am drained,

I am so stressed that my hair is falling out. I can't be your image of perfect anymore. I have forced myself to dream your dream. I tried for so long to be everything you needed and wanted me to be, but I can't. This life is way too short. I already wasted 21 years of my life doing what was expected of me, and now I want to do *nothing* that is expected of me. I am tired of not caring for organic chemistry, but having to do it. When you love someone, you will do anything to make them happy, but at some point I have to make myself happy. I know you are mad, or more so furious, but I hope you can respect my decision. I don't want to be a doctor." And as Life finished, she took her one piece of baggage, left her parents' house, and scratched her head under her favorite orange hat. As she pulled her hand from it, a clump of hair fell from the sky of her head and she began to tear up. She hoped it was just the stress again.

When she reached the nearest train to head into the city, she stopped. She looked up and exhaled. Then, she began walking onto the most packed train she had ever seen (it was so packed, that what do people call it? Packed like sardines?) Well, they were that. She worked her way around multiple people in an attempt to find a seat, and as she reached the last car of the train, Voila! There it was. A seat sitting next to a boring-looking 27-year-old man with a Bluetooth in one ear, one headphone in the other, and a cell phone that was viciously getting beaten by his fingers. He had a caramel complexion, and wore the most uppity business suit she had ever seen. It was 8 PM. He could have at least loosened his tie, but no. He wore it choked up to his neck, almost too perfectly.

Life walked up to the seat and said very politely, "Excuse me, do you mind if I sit here?"

His three pieces of electronics drowned out her voice. So, she began to blatantly cough.

He did not turn.

She spoke a little louder, "Excuse me, can you move your jacket so that I can sit?"

Still no response.

So, with one arm holding the seat, she pretended like she was choking.

He turned quickly, froze, and then immediately moved his jacket. He removed every electronic that separated them just a little bit more.

He let her sit and they began to talk.

He usually knew exactly what to say to make a woman smile. He always had the perfect pickup lines waiting in the back of his head, like, "For a moment I thought I had died and gone to heaven. Now I see that I am very much alive, and heaven has been brought to me." But, he didn't need words with her. Their connection was unreal, it was beyond earthly. It was like they knew each other from another life and were simply continuing their love.

After about five stops, he realized she was beginning to pick up her luggage and button her jacket, so he began to cough.

She ignored him with a growing smirk.
He coughed a bit more obnoxiously three more times. She slowly turned her head, fixed her hat and said, "Do you need a cough drop, sir?"

As he turned red, he smiled and said, "Um. No thank you. But, I did notice that you are getting ready to get off the train soon and I was wondering if you would like to go out with me sometime?"
She smirked again and fixed her hat. As they exchanged names and numbers, she contemplated giving him a fake number, but she then remembered what it felt like not to be loved, and what she felt during the past half hour with him felt nothing like that. She figured that she should at least give it a try.

After the first date of catching fireflies on an open field, turned into five dates, she knew this was something real. She knew that life was not only about running, and jumping, and hiking, but about love. Life is meaningless without love, and life slowly begins to deteriorate without it. Without Love, Life is empty, it is lonely, and heavy. Love is put in this world to remind us that the world is a paradox. It is heaven and hell wrapped into one, but it holds us so well in it. Love is laying on that person's chest and holding your breath over and over again in attempt to intertwine two hearts. Love is two straws in one drink. Love is the little things and those little things are what tell us that

Life is worth living.

As their fifth date was coming to an end that evening, he walked her to the door. He began to lean in for a kiss, and she stopped him. She said, "Come with me." She walked him into the middle of the street, and as they stood under a glowing streetlight, she gave him her breath. Then she began to dance (I told you she was wild).

As he walked her back to her door, he thought to himself how Life was his supernova, an exploding bundle of energy, unexpected, and extreme. She was the wild woman to his reserved.

He held her tight before he built the courage to turn around and leave. She entered her house and as the door slowly shut behind her, she began to feel dizzy. She took one step. The next step was a little bit shorter in stride and Life fell to the ground. She called for her roommate, who ran to her, asking what happened. Life was unconscious. She took Life's hat off to give her some air and noticed that Life had approximately seven bald spots, and with her hair thinning, she left a trail of herself everywhere she went.

Life knew that she couldn't hold onto this new love, while she was going through such a crazy time in her life. She knew that he deserved someone better, a "normal" girl, someone who didn't have to worry about him trying to run his fingers through her hat instead of her hair, or if he was strong enough to fight with her and for her.

As the ambulance came and took her away, Life's roommate sat right next to her. Life said,

"Promise that you won't tell him anything. I am OK. The next time I see him I will end things with him." She agreed and they pinky swore.

Life knew that without him, she had nothing to live for. She pushed away the one thing that would be unconditional. She needed help, and she wouldn't let him save her. When Life is missing love, she is lost. She is very, very lost. Life without love is unnatural. It is not a life at all; it is separated, and cold. It is a rainbow in black and white, a face without the option to smile. Life needs love in order to *be*, and she pushed it away; far, far away, because she did not want to hurt him.

They had not spoken in almost a month and Life was beginning to get weaker and weaker. She just laid in the hospital bed, and awaited more medicine to numb whatever feeling was left. Her roommate barely ever left; she was there at lunch time and stayed till midnight. Whenever she'd come back in the afternoon, she would bring Life all of the flowers that were sent to the house, and all of the love letters that were sent apologizing for that night (It is interesting when a person apologizes for something that both people know was perfect). Life smelled every flower, read every letter, and answered each letter in her head. She could not get herself to tell him why she ignores him every day and really ended things. She knew she had hurt him, but knowing the truth, that she may die … would hurt him so much more.

Pocket Full of Poems I
Life.

Prideless.

He is *that* guy.
The guy everyone shakes their head at.
Laughs at uncomfortably.
Rolls eyes at.
And sucks their teeth at.
But, refuses to make eye contact with because maybe
he'll go away.
Because eye contact creates a connection.
A feeling.
And you can't ignore feelings.

He's the one we always have an excuse for.
Who we lie to,
So easily lie to because he is nothing but a stranger
whose hardest job is begging.
He's the one who begs for change and says, "That's all
you got?"

Don't be picky with my generosity.

He is the one who had a name.
Who was like you and me.
He's the one with Miller-stained breath,
A stumble in his walk from keeping five dollars in
change as cushion in ripped-toed brown loafers, and
has black dirt in bitten, low nails.

He gets hungry sometimes.

He's the 40-, maybe 45-year-old man who uses store
windows to check if he has any bits of pride left in his
teeth,
cuts his beard with grade school scissors,
and eats what we're too full to finish.

He is the one who chews on his last 1929 Castiano
cigar to taste the better days of jazz clubs,
And bourbon,
And grandfather clocks.

He mumbles, "Time goes too fast."

Too fast at times.

He's the man who makes loud noises to test which
woman has enough care he can take.
He calls me "sweet thang."
I ignore his advances and say
"Do right with my dollar."

Ignoring is easier than forgetting.

So I move my purse.
I always move my purse.
Because this homeless man,
His kind,
With only regret scratching the back of his throat,
And anger wallowing deep in his heart.

His kind, makes it hard for every other homeless man
and woman standing on the poverty line who actually
need my pocket change for more than a beer.

I've come to avoid all connections.
I have given up hope.

I just shake my head.
Laugh uncomfortably.
Roll my eyes.
And suck my teeth.
Assuming, all will be just like him.

Narrate Me in Nostalgia

Rita was so brittle.

She was stained of sleepless nights and "I love yous" painted on chipped fingernails.

Little boy wrapped tight in her chocolate arms.

She never knew that love could not be equally split in two.

So, the other.

The older son sat on the frigid stainless steel subway bench furthest from her heart.

"I know that my mom loves me, but can't express it totally. She has to be strong for the little bro.

That's why I just sit, shut up, and draw.

My mom says that I have my pop's eyes—the first time she met him—big eyes that can see the world.

I draw this world with melted crayon and paint my smiles on a canvas of wishful thinking, in hopes of making all of this dark in the world light again.

And everything goes away."

"Mommy loves me more than you! I'm her favorite! NA NA NA BOO BOO!

My big brother is as quiet as a fox.

But, also as quiet as this cat I saw on our neighbor's

lawn, sort of like Batman.

Wait! Batman isn't a cat though. (Giggles)

Welp, anywhoozer! They both are really, really quiet and sort of sit there like the roadkill I saw on the street one day after this huge-gungeous truck ran over it … and do nothing.

EXCEPT Batman because he saves GOTHAM CITY! …

Mommy loves me more than you!"

"Nah. They're not my kids.

Yeah, yeah, yeah, you were my girlfriend and whatever, but they're not mine.

You're strong.

You got it, woman.

You want me to do something?

Here.

Here's a subway Metro card.

I used it once, there should be three swipes left for y'all.

Enjoy."

Prince Charming

His mommy always told him that one day he will
shine as bright as the moon,
That one day he will be a king.
Imagine if he could have flown when he jumped?
Tinkerbell twirling wings sprouting from his back,
cracking the notches in his spine into pitch black,
he was soaring along the skyline of his spellbinding
smile.

I always wondered what gay men wish for among the
stars?
Do they dream that fairy tales apply to every type of
love?
Does he sit and wait until castles blink open,
let down his long hair and have his knight in shining
armor rescue him?
For him to bite a poisonous fruit sleeping handsomely
and awaken the heaven in his breath with his true
love's lips upon his face.
To waltz with a beast
and live happily ever after with a prince found in a
frog.

His mommy always told him that he will one day
shine as bright as the moon.
That one day he will be a King,
but Kings can't play dress-up these days.
Yet, kings blushed like 4-year-old little boys playing
in mommy's makeup.
But a queen trapped as a king is beaten
with frying pans and metal rods echoing like drums,

sounding like the trumpets singing, townspeople
calling for their King.
He is beautiful.

Gwen "Eddie" Arajuo and Matthew Sheppard loved to
play dress-up.
Bobby Griffith and Tyler Clementi wondered,
with magical fairy dust sprinkled up on top, if they'd
fly like Peter Pan off of broken bridges.
For all they craved was knowing if the world was still
flat or
if an enchanted sun pop-up-booked to kiss the moon.
Does this world still kiss with their eyes closed?
Dance like seven dwarfs.
Pray to a genie or the fairy godmother of gods that my
love cannot be taken.
So, fairy godmother, I seek to ask you to grant me one
wish, even if only until the clock strikes 12.

For one night let love be in safekeeping,
rid this world of every evil stepmother,
every strangling weed in a blushing heart,
and every word the size of fists, and every fist the size
of pumpkins that can carriage him away.
And let him step upon that ledge.
Take a jump and fly away to Never Land.

My mommy always used to read me a bedtime story.
A story of a man who shined as bright as the moon.
Angel wings sprouting from his back,
cracking the notches in his spine into pitch black.
I dreamed of a Queen.

Beethoven's Last Song

There is a symphony playing in Justin's head.

Music.

Notes that only Bach would waste the motion in his fingers on.

Music,

That, "normal people," their ears are not fit to hear.

According to doctors, Justin is broken.
They say, the day he was born, he was too mute.
That the only reason he reached for his mother was because he felt a beat; it was something as beautiful as Beethoven, he could wiggle his fingers too.

At two months old, Justin was diagnosed with autism.

He will never see this world from our eyes.
He may never realize if he hurts you when he walks away while you're still speaking.
He may never taste the sweet words from a woman's mouth.

Justin is *different*.

According to doctors, *different* needs to be fixed,
different is a disease,
different is being too simple

because life must be complex,
but Justin is beautiful.
Simply beautiful.

For if not for music, we might in these days say that
beautiful is dead, but every time Justin tickles a key on
the grand piano, it gives Beethoven a second chance at
life.

The first time I hung out with Justin, a Waka Flocka
Flame song was bumping in the background.
I asked,
        "Do you like this whole gangster rap flow?"

He covered his ears, and said
                                        "No."

        Then began humming *Moonlight Sonata*.
I stopped listening to lyrics because of hip-hop and
began listening to a sweet song, as sweet as a spring-
time-sweet symphony that only the soul alone can
comprehend, but will never be capable of translating.
When you see a person's soul for the very first time, it
is as breathtaking as the moment before a first kiss.

                        Justin takes my breath away.
When he is performing,
He   is performing,
He is not   performing for you,
                        for me,
                        or a medal that only hugs him
in past tense.

There is no, "was he good enough?" when there is no distraction of trying to be good enough.

Justin is great enough and he doesn't even care,

Justin is great enough,

Justin is great enough.

When Justin did not win the gold medal in a national competition all he said was,

"I am hungry."

He is the *enough* that we ignore.

Justin has taught himself Spanish in his spare time.
He wears glasses as thick as his mother's skin.
He loves to sing Beyonce's "Love on Top."

His mother called him a miracle.
But miracles are surprises.

God knew what He was blessing this earth with.

My Father

My father is a Warrior.
He will set peace free from its cage tonight.
My father is a Captain.
My father is my family's lighthouse.
My father is a bull with a heart as sweet as red.
My father is a Gladiator.
My father is the Colosseum ruins.
He still stands after years of battle.
My father is a story of hope.

My father has fought the lions for me tonight.
My father is a king. He calls me his princess.
My father is music.
I have never heard music until I laid on my father's
chest when I was six years young.
His heart beats.
I think when I closed my eyes I dreamt of Ellington
and Gillespie sitting at a table for 3 with my father
My father is history.
Not just Black History.
But a story too loud for one page in a book.

My father is a man and a man is what he reads,
what he sees,
what he does,
what he is.
My father is a southern summertime smile.
My father realized how much power rests in that
crescent shape when he met my mother on her saddest
day and cracked, blossom- bloomed open that fault

line in her smile.
They are 22 again.

My father is power.
My father is love.
My father hates no one.
My father hated my 13-year old boyfriend.
My father is stubborn.
My father is the truth we can't explain.
My father is the truth we call this earth.
His eyelashes bat like a butterfly taking in its first
breath.
My father has breathed in more days than he has
thanked God for.
I thank God for him.
My father gets older but his voice gets stronger.
My father has a voice of a train engine.
My father never stops.
My father has never gone.
My father is my Papito, and my Papito is my daddy.

My dad is strength.
My dad doesn't always have to be strong but my dad, I
have never seen my dad cry,
but my dad is a rain cloud pulling itself back so that
the sun can come out to play for his children.
My dad is that oak of a tree in our backyard we used to
climb as kids.
My dad has never fallen down, but if I saw my dad
cry...I would look up to him more.
My dad has hands like a hammock, carrying my
weight on his back.

My dad has hands that can hold up my world.
My dad is one of the seven wonders of my world.
My dad is a martyr.
My dad questions.
My dad knocks.
My dad is the answer.
My dad is the pen I wrote this poem in.
My dad will make this poem legendary.
My dad is legendary.

Grandma's House

It reeked of jungle.

Jurassically aged, dinosaur serpent giant

it,

this Grandfather-like Brussels sprout devoured us alive
as our feet applauded its bark.

Weeds weeded itself around its cocky arms
like ex-lovers' one-night stand, it reeked of jungle.

Tarantula legs weaving inside and out,

frightened of vampire fangs lusting for our skins.

This bushing, blushing, beanstalk was a playground
turning into a zombie.

The night rewrote days tasting of shadows, while
golly-gee green giants heartlessly

strangled itself to death and we climbed forever.

STOP TALKING

I will strip Webster's Dictionary for you.

Tap dance on the alphabet and concoct our own
language. A language only written in the   heavens of
the underworld because words switch us mute, yet
words are air,

a relapsing creative attempt to breathe our thoughts.
Let us
speak in tongues.

Ramen Noodles

My brother refuses to date a woman whose hair
reminds him of our mother.
He says that he doesn't date black girls because their
hair is too greasy,
their naps keep his fingers from running through their
strands, because their strands
rather hold onto the burnt smell of a flat iron than the
scent of him.
Because all of the real gets sweated out.
None of it's real.
My brother thinks that he knows it all
That he knows how it feels to be examined on
sidewalks,
Rated from 1 to 10, and 10 never scratching the
surface of a man's mind because
we'll never be his perfection.
Compared to every basketball wife and wife that gets
paid off of "*How beautiful can they make beauty?*"

He thinks he knows the cure to fixing us.
It's ironic.
If our hair only dandelion blew in the wind, we'd be a
tad bit prettier
but, our hair is the weed blossoming through the
cracks of our scalp.
Face it, they want us to believe we were built ugly.

That we need 500-dollar weaves to fulfill our men's
false Barbie perceptions of an African queen.

But in truth, we're making our men feel comfortable
that they can say they are dating a mixed woman

versus a black woman …
There is a three-island orgy up in this mane.
There are 400 years of history in your mane.
We are all mixed.

In the past 20 years, I can count on one hand how
many times my brother has called me beautiful.
And I have always given him an excuse for why he
couldn't, because he was right.
All I had to do was nitpick, and
cut and clip, and
tuck and tighten because
I can always be prettier.
I can always be prettier.
I can always be prettier.

His words are a part of me.
This world's words are a part of us.
Staying with us.
Dead words, buried so deep like a skeleton attached to
an ever-evolving coral reef.
These words are in our bones.

So to my brother:
Our mother will forever be the elementary school love
letter given to you by a little black girl with naps
wrapped in dip 'n' dot hair clips and bows that was
easier to answer buried in sand than to simply check
no.

You were always so good at not facing the truth.

Our mother will be that rusted family photograph you
place under your bed mattress when women with hair
like silk come to taste the insecure in your skin,

that water-stained ring in the mahogany of your
kitchen table,
You have tried to scrub our mother out of you.
You are a bag of stones.
Heavy and rough.
There is wicker in your smile.

and I am so sorry for whoever hurt you.

But, I am not these curly locks that'd rather stand up
for a statement than fall across my forehead.
I am not my hair.
You are not your hair.

We are all just a pile of lovely bones dying to be loved
gorgeous.

Part II

Love.
It is OK to have a broken Heart.
It means you have Given.
-Alyea Pierce

I met Love on a Sunday train.

He was 6'1" on a good day and with good shoes, and wore a business suit almost too perfectly. He spoke Spanglish beautifully, had a delicate caramel complexion, and no comprehension of what a smile could actually accomplish. He was a workaholic (someone must love work if they *choose* to work on a Sunday). His back stood as straight as an ironing board. He had a cell phone in his left hand, a tablet in his lap, a Bluetooth in his right ear, and one headphone in his left ear, which connected to his laptop that stood on top of his briefcase, lying on the seat next to him. Some would say he was connected; however, he was the most disconnected person on that train ride.

Love wasn't always like this.

He remembers when love meant enjoying the way she moves and not asking for more. When it was important to listen for more than himself. He remembers when love was freeing, when love was an attachment. How it was a damn contradiction. He remembers when love was the magic trick that lit his eyes like two jars of caught fireflies. He remembers when love was knowing that some things in this life

34

are impossible, but knowing that in Life's arms, he would keep trying. He remembers trying to bite her palm (go ahead, try). Love was living. Love was living. Love was living. Love was the scariest adventure. Love was a broken law. He remembers being 15 years old, and sneaking outside of his parents' home before the moon woke the sun, just to breathe in morning with another stranger turned lover. He remembers being 20 years old, and listening to Bob Marley's "Is this Love" on a swing set until she fell asleep in the corner of his arm. As much as his arm fell asleep, he never once moved. He remembers being 27 years old, waking up next to Life and not getting up because the sun was intruding on a lover's night. He remembers when Life took three months of his life and showed him the level of happiness that could be achieved when a person gives a stranger a chance. She was whimsical; had a meek, yet sassy heart and always wore her hair short with that orange hat topping it off. They enjoyed each other.

Love remembers the moment Life pulled away.

It was 4 AM, the Tuesday after Labor day, two Tuesdays after she came back from the hospital, and they were sleeping in her bed, packed with pillows. Life loved pillows, and Love hated it. Love hated how she laid every pretty little pillow perfectly every morning, just to get messed up every evening. But, he knew that a made bed reminded her that the little things are what make a lover happy.

That night she was different. Life normally

moves throughout the entire night, kicking pillows onto the floor, stealing covers, but that night, she stood still. She laid on her back, with eyes open.

Love asked, "Babe, you good? You usually have kicked me or taken all of the covers by now." He began to chuckle.

She said nothing.

"Babe?"

He placed his palm to her chin and turned her face to him. He looked at her.
Tears running from her eyes.

He asked. "What's wrong? Have you been awake crying next to me the whole night? What—"

He didn't know what to say. He knew his arms could speak louder than any question, so he hugged her as tight as he could, but she thought it would be easier if she didn't hold him back.
She pushed herself away, and looked him in his eyes. With puddles filling her eyes again, she could not hold the overflow of water back. The tears continued to stream down her face.

She suddenly sat up and said, "You deserve more than this, and I want you to be happy even if it's without me."
"Huh?"

"You heard me. Promise me that you will be happy even without me? Please!"

"Babe? I am really confused. Where is this coming from?"

"Just say you will. I need to hear you say that, please, you won't understand, please!"

He never heard her beg before. He did not know where this was going, so he began with, "No. I won't promise you something like that. I want you and only you, and that's that. If you think I won't understand, make me understand. I am here wanting to, and you're not giving me the chance to and why would I lie to myself or you by promising that I will be happy with someone else? You are what makes me happy."

His non-compliance led her to her third stance within this conversation. She now stood, with folded arms. He knew she was holding something from him, but he could not figure it out. Life began to get really frustrated and said, "If you knew how much I loved you, you would understand why I did this!"

She grabbed his stuff and threw it onto the bed, implying that it was time for him to go.

"Why are you doing this, please tell me what is going on? This isn't like you!"

"Leave, please." She couldn't look him in the eyes as

he approached the door and closed all of what could have been behind him.

After one week of sending flowers, knocking on her door, and receiving no response, he stopped. After three weeks of sending handwritten letters apologizing for not listening that night and receiving no response, he stopped. After four weeks of crying and receiving no response, he stopped.

Although she never left his mind, he tried to put her closer to the back of it, until he randomly received a letter from her roommate in the mail. It stated that he needed to come to the hospital, room 727, that night. It said that all of his questions would be answered. It ended with "Trust me, please."

As the elevator numbers climbed up to seven, his heart started racing. He called the roommate and she met him at the entrance of the seventh floor. She started the conversation with, "She doesn't know you are coming; she doesn't even want you to see her like this, but I had to. The doctors said that she only had one month to live, but she surpassed that."

He was confused. But as he started walking down the hallway, the word cancer began to scream at him from every which way. He finally understood where she was taking him when he saw a little girl wearing the same exact orange crochet hat Life always wore.

Room 725.

Room 726.

"Here we are. Go in quietly, I will wait out here." The

roommate walked away.

He walked in slowly and began tearing up when he saw her. Life was pale, nearly 100 pounds of bone, skin and heart, and was plugged into the wall. It made sense why she always wore that orange hat now. As he reached the side of her bed, he grabbed her hand and said "Babe."

She looked up and said "No. No. No. No. No."

"Stop. I am here. I know. I see now."

"You were supposed to remember me beautiful. Not like this."

"You are beautiful."

Tears poured from her eyes. "I never meant to hurt you. I didn't want to drag you—"

He quieted her and said, "It doesn't matter now."

"No. Let me finish because I don't know how much time I have left. The doctors have a new number every day. I didn't want to drag you along on this journey with me. It's pain, it's not pretty. Was that selfish? Was that my decision to make?"

"Babe, please stop."

"I didn't want to take anything from your life. I wanted you to remember the good times and never have to worry."

With his voice quivering he said, "If only you knew that you did take something from me. You took my heart from the moment I saw you and I never wanted you to give it back to me. That night, you took my best friend from me, you took my lover, and you never gave me the chance to be there for you. But, I am here now. I am not leaving you."

"They said I only had one month to live. I am onto a new month, but I am tired. I am so tired; these machines, and these meds, and this chemo are taking the life from me."

He did not know what to say. He just put his head to her chest and listened to her heart beat. He kept holding his breath so that maybe their hearts could beat in unison, and every few beats, it did. When he said that he would never leave her, he didn't. He was there every day.

Love remembers how desperately Life needed saving. How desperate Life needed Love but pushed it away, far, far away. Love remembers when the doctors began counting down how long she would have left to live into weeks, then hours, then minutes. The doctors didn't need to count down the seconds. Love remembers that. Love remembers how angry he was. He remembers how angry he was that someone could put a number to someone's life. He remembers how mad he was at her. He remembers lying in his dark apartment by himself and questioning if his heart should stay. Love would never leave Life. Love knew that this was not the end. Love remembers thinking that this may have to be the end. Love remembers questioning who would create a human to feel such pain. Love remembers waiting for her to awaken.

Love remembers when Life left.

He keeps her favorite pillow, at the center of his made bed every morning, and sleeps with it, messing up the beauty of such a simple thing every evening. He loves one or two pillows now (I guess people do rub off on one another).

Love is lost. Love has been missing something since Life left. Love is at a loss without Life. He became stagnant, separated, left on a broken train track. Love is lost because he compares every woman to Life.

But they are never her.

Love makes sure to give as little of himself as he can when he says his first name over two martinis. Love lives through the physical. He blocks out the world by listening to Beethoven's 5th symphony on repeat, and reminiscing on the women he never called back. Love loves love in that moment. He loves to touch, and feel, and stain these women's skin, but he remembers what Life taught him: that not touching is sometimes the only way to know true love. He is terrified of what could actually be again.

The train was packed (It was so packed, that

what do people call it? Packed like sardines, I think.)
Well, we were that and this 27-year-old man allowed
his excess baggage of supposed business to be his
excuse for no one to get too close. But when I walked
on that train with my hands full of baggage from last
night's trip from the city, there was only one seat
open. The one next to him, which everyone stood
around because they feared intruding on the wall Love
built up.

I slowly walked up to the seat and said, "Excuse me,
do you mind if I sit here?"

His 50 pieces of electronics drowned out my voice.
I began to blatantly cough.

He did not turn.

I spoke a little louder, "Excuse me, do you mind if I
move your things?"

No response.

So, with one arm holding the seat, I pretended like I
was choking.

He turned quickly and then froze.

I did not know if the hacking up of my heart scared
him, or reminded him of someone else who tried to get
his attention.
But, he let me sit.

He put all of his electronics away and stared at me. His eyes said that he was waiting for me to say that this was a joke, but I didn't and he didn't.

Instead he turned to me and gave me something. He gave me Words. He asked, "Have you ever been in love?"

I replied, "No. Nothing I would consider *love*."

"Remember this then: Love can unknowingly, drastically and hopefully change every cell in your body. Allow it to infect your body for the better." His eyes began to gloss over.

He turned back to the window, took out all of his gadgets once again, and separated himself from the world one more time.

Love is infected with love, but he only has it in the spiritual, and that infuriates him. He knows that she is in the air, cloud-surfing, and telling the world to stop worrying so much. He misses her, and now all he has left is giving people all the words Life taught him and living through all of the fairy tales, movies, and stories about butterflies being caught in stomachs. Life was the exception and love was an expectation. It was everything Love was told it should be, but now, he has forgotten how to feel.

Pocket Full of Poems II
Love.

Him

Sunday mornings taste like sugar.

Those Sunday mornings before you let time take you away.

Those mornings when you traced the lifelines in my palms between wedding white sheets in an attempt to read how long our love would live in the palms of my hands.

I used to wonder, what my mind would look like with no memory of you.

Would it be black or look like the word *lonely*;

Would it be better off?

Would you pop up in my dreams because my subconscious knows better?

Because it knows you are a part of me?

No matter if the memory of you looks better in someone else's mind.

If forgetting you was as easy as blinking,
I'd fear closing my eyes for too long.

Because for too long I thought I was not worthy of sharing the same pillow with an image of God.

A bed built of feathers plucked from the bone of

angels' wings,
We are so fortunate to have a piece of heaven in our world.

You have given me love, and
my goal is to annoy you for the rest of our lives.
You.
Right here with me.
And me.
Right here with you.
Face to face.
I close my eyes and inhale your truth.

You are a lotus flower cracking bloom for the very first time, and I,
like a little child entranced by your beauty, will never pick the petals from your smile.
I can only stare in awe that I have been able to lay my hand upon a living garden.

I will swim in my thoughts with you and not in such empty words to tell you how crazy you make me feel.

I will show you like you are the lost piece to God's puzzle and I am your lighthouse.
Shining just for you.
I have been searching the lengths of the sea and until the clock strikes 13 just for you,
For you to make a home in this barren tower of a heart.

Let me sing you the oldest-known love song,

that sits on the river's floor of Tigris and Euphrates,

and although I am a fool with no capabilities of holding a tune,

45

Seeing you shake your head and your nose crinkle in embarrassment makes me appreciate you that much more.
Because you are still here with me.

But, I am absolutely terrified to let all of me love you and

I want you to be the last person I introduce my heart to.

I want to Love you hard,

as hard as it was to not put your name in this poem.

Love you as hard as a first kiss after being a year of an ocean ways apart.

Love you because you were the unexpected event that I could not run my game on.

You were that unexpected event that made me

run the opposite direction.

But you caught me,

You catch me every time.

I have written a hundred love poems for you.

Some for our past, a few more for all that we aren't …

and the rest are for all that we could ever be.

I hope one day,

On a Sunday morning tasting like sugar,

                                        You'll listen.

There's No Place like Home

The gods painted a mural of us last night.

They mixed sweet sunset colors with midsummer night,

dipped the ring of their fingers in tomorrow's rainbow and

brushed it along our blank canvas.

They laid a large checkerboard cloth upon a park's floor, so we could play a game of chess with our hearts

But, I let him win.

I whispered, "Play dead" in my rooks and he passed that message along like a game of telephone to the knight and the pawns, just so that this man could take me as his queen without war.

The gods sketched his curly brown hair as a fresh Brillo pad.

Reminding him of all the childhood nicknames that always left him as "just a friend,"

nicknames that always lasted four years longer than they ever should.

But, not today.

Not in my arms.

Because he is my definition of beauty.

He caressed my ears with each word he chose, and

he never let his metaphors let go of me.

He held me tight, as tight as a wedding band hugs a
ring finger.

He never let me go.

He crawled his hand over to mine and intertwined our
pinkies.

We can hold one another until every piece dies and we
no longer have a place for our picnics.

The gods allowed us to see a glimpse of perfection that
day.

They painted a masterpiece.

Grandfather

I knew since I was a little girl,

I wanted to die in the hands of the ocean's air,

warm yet slightly clammy like nervous palms.

I knew it could stutter shock "I love you" over my empty heartbeat and awaken my love.

I knew since I was a little girl,

I wanted to die in the hands of the ocean's air,

warm yet slightly clammy,

your hands could sail over that blushing curve of my ribs on that 18th night of November.

I knew you weren't the one.

The day you reminded me of my grandfather.

His palms never cried of nostalgia a day in his life for my grandmother,

never yelled "I love you" at the top of his fingertips, or, "You are beyond this beauty we speak of."

He spoke in silence.

Silence does not speak louder than words.

It is an excuse.

If the only thing that makes all of this emptiness

bearable is each other,

Then why do we fear stepping on the cracks of our smiles.

We are all big bug-eyed people craving for that symphony of choreographed fairy tales,

Tales telling the remnants of us gladiators who dare to inhale this human love.

Love is selfish.

Compliment me.

Love is selfish.

Hold me.

Love is selfish.

Do you feel me? Do you see me? Do you hear me?

We don't want to speak through poems anymore.

I knew since I was 16, I wanted my man to cry.

Taste his tears like water and skip rocks on the rivers of his spine.

I knew you weren't the one,

the day you hugged me two seconds too short,

wiped your face when you saw me reach for your hand, and

every broken limb ripped off daisies landed on "I love you not."

My grandmother told me a story once.

Of the crisp morning my grandfather blinked for the final time,

like 10,000 grains of sand kissing "I will see you soon" off retinas,

he died in her arms.

Her palms cried like Frank Sinatra's voice dipped in piano men and brandy,

Then silence.

I guess it's not an excuse.

I always thought love echoed only through words,

but that night I dreamed of darkness and saw a single candle lit in the center of all of this black.

You see, the way the cosmos fit into that one grain of light,

expecting nothing in return,

is so much more than the lifelessness in his love. You can feel the Temptation doo-wops as incense dance on the bridge of your nose,

The burning smoke is dying to smell another being before the air takes it hostage.

The silent beauty a secret screams is so much more than three hallowed words,

It is grace.

I knew since I was a little girl I wanted to taste heaven right here on earth.

I'll wait for that day,

and love louder than a deaf man's hands.

10x10

The space between their words was as empty
as the cracked suburban road they watched black
ants roam aimlessly on before he left. She
sweated tears on fried egg sidewalks waiting
for the mailman to send her love's love. But,
it always rained on Sunday. Love never
came. The space between their space was as dis-
tant, as the distance from ear to ear.
He never heard the ripples of her
"I Need You's" beating dead air. Need. You. Now.

Curiosity Tastes like You

He is the sun shower she's wanted to jump into, but
instead gazed at through windows.
Glass is cold.
And her palms hug the outside so well through it.
She stands next to that chance,
that "what if,"
for she fears it becomes as lonely as her.

I Write Not to Love

Contradiction was the underbelly of our breath.

"I love you but … "

"I miss you but … "

"I know what I want, but I know what I need."

I am not an easy woman to want.

I fall in love with the idea of love

     So.

          Damn.

               Easy.

The first time we kissed was the last time we made love and

          I haven't heard from him since.

He would never guess that the spotlight makes me nervous, but

standing naked in front of a mic,

throwing my diary at a mic is vulnerable.

Standing naked in front of him,

throwing myself at him is vulnerable.

Vulnerable, is a naked word many women don't practice,

but I've practiced confessing my love to him

in journals,

in mirrors,

and in people

too many times that this should be too easy.

But, love is never as easy as a poem.

The person you want to hear the poem never really
hears the poem

We're both not ready to hear this poem.

He says that I am never here.

But he is never here the way I need him to be here.

We are both never really here even when we are
standing in the same room.

We both only hear and hearing is never enough.

We both only hear and never just

                                  Listen.

His love for me is the decrescendo of a music box.

The ballerina slowly turning into standstill.

The knob at its last

                        click, before there is nothing left
but   silence.

Summer

Under the summer's moon,

She danced cheek to cheek alongside her balloon.
"Men don't know how to dance on air,"

somersault beneath arms, and two-step without any
step at all.

"A man," she says,

"Holds her back" from dancing on platinum stars
majestically stretched out on
New York "I dream a dream" skylines, waltzing
on luxurious mountains, and mamboing on Niagara
Falls mist.

"A man" she claims,

        does not know how to
moonwalk his fingers across the grooves in her spine,
but
a balloon does.

She says,   he doesn't know
how to jive to the silent heartbeat of Mars,

quickstep on the Palisades Sill,
and
samba with aurora borealis from dawn till dusk.

She and her balloon can
slow dance like Giants and line-dance up pomegranate

56

beanstalks.

Paso Doble to the top of the bell tower,

Ring her Bell.
And if her balloon dwindles of breath she will become
hunchbacked,

Notre Dame will be forever dancing in her ethereal
arms.

"So dance with me," she says.
"Balloon dance with me" gracefully on soft
marshmallow-roasted nebulas, swing
on the aged line of Mount Rushmore.

"Dance with me," she cries.

Her balloon does not make a face,

                           does not chuckle
when she steps on the space between their feet.
She is a child,
               jumping
into its arms like a little girl taking sail on a merry go
round,
                spinning forever
in a golden-gemmed world,
not knowing that this room of ballroom-dancing
beauties and beasts will stop turning one day.
But,
for now it goes slowly, slowly
turning,

and she smiles.
Cracking the earth of her lips into the San Andreas
Fault, and

                                            lets her balloon go.

        Letting it fly away to dance on Mars alone.

Wallflowers Do Blossom

When the shadows overtake the sun and we slow
dance, our hearts strum the strings

of our rib cages, and

my cheeks rust into a crimson blush.

Let's move.

Like a deaf man's hands drawing snow angels on air. I
want to dance on air, or at least stand on your feet.

Speaking through our bodies give reason to no longer
wish on daisies,

or dream on a swelled sky, prayer full.

So, let's take that stroll in the Central Park of our
souls, and turn poetry into pirouettes.

Take my hand.

Take.

My.

Hand.

This last dance was saved for you because dancing
never dies out and a rhythm lives on forever.

Part III

Loss.

It takes losing everything, to realize all that we are.
-Alyea Pierce

I bumped into her accidentally.
I was coming off the train,
headed home, and then I accidentally bumped into her.
She stopped.
She didn't keep walking and roll her eyes, like every
other stranger I've bumped into in the past did.
She was different;
she stopped,
in the middle of the busiest crossing.
She stopped and so did I, curious and dumbfounded
that she did not have something better to do than stare
at me in the middle of the road during rush hour.
We continued to stare.
Her, with no emotion.
Me, terrified because our pedestrian crossing sign
switched to "Do Not Walk."
She continued to stare at me.
Then, the light perpendicular to us switched to yellow.
I got nervous. (I always know when I get nervous
because I unconsciously wipe my sweaty palms on the
side of my jeans three times; it is a habit.)

Drivers began to honk and edge closer to the walkway
that I thought could save us.
Then it jumped to red.
I yelled "MOVE!" as she stood frozen … still staring.
The light on our side snapped to green.

I grabbed her.

And that is how I met Loss.

Loss was brown-haired with soft highlights of gold, glasses that oozed sexy librarian, and in her late 20s'. Her eyes were a foggy gray, glazed over like rain had fallen from them too many times today. Clothes? I could tell she was the kind of girl that liked to hide in his baggy sweatshirts. She felt safe there for two and a half years. But he took them all when he left, one month ago today. He ended it with her. It wasn't easy to end things for him because it is never easy, but he let frustration take control of feeling. He said she was changing on her own, and not evolving with him. She wasn't the girl he met the first day of college, the first time he understood that co-ed really means that the girl of his dreams can literally live next door.

Loss was beautiful. Skin glowing like grandma's china because there was purpose in grandma's china; it was something to take care of. But, I knew as beautiful as she was, she was empty.

I knew she was not only lost amongst pedestrian traffic and crowds of strangers, but she had no more care left in her. No more heart. No more energy left in her eyes. I couldn't understand how someone could be so low.

The human in me wanted to relate, but I couldn't.

We walked to the nearest coffee shop and sat on the bar stools facing the window to the outside. I thought that after a young stranger was about to commit suicide, especially in front of me, the least I could do was listen.

I let her choose the seat.
        She continued to look outside and rarely ever at me. She liked to look at how the strangers maneuvered themselves around one another, making sure not to touch, not to make eye contact. She noticed how the strangers she watched either looked down or straight ahead, never up where hope and faith lingers. She realized how her boyfriend of two and a half years never looked up.

As she spoke to the air in a whisper, her first words went something like this…

"If I was happy,
would you live in this moment with me?"

"Um, yes I—" I began.

"Huh? I am not even talking to you," she said.

"Well, I mean, I am the only one with you in this coffee shop, so I assumed—"

"See, that's everyone's problem. Assumptions. If I need you to be my superhero, I will let you know…"
She shook her head and began to calm down.

I shook my head and began fiddling with a puddle of leftover coffee on the counter.

I let her finish whispering to herself.

"If I cried,
would you hold me?

"If I was scared,
would you protect me?

"If I was in need,
would you hold my hand?

"If I was lost,
would you find me?

"If I died,
would you even notice?

"Would you even care? … Because I am nothing but a stranger to you.

"Don't lie. Would you?"

My head snapped up and I hesitated to speak. "You're speaking to me? I can answer now?"

She gave me an evil eye.

Still with hesitation, I answered,
"Um …
"Yes, I would do all of those things. I would live in this moment with you, I would hold you, and protect you. I would find you, and notice. Yes. Of course I

would notice even if you are nobody in my life. "Even if you are a stranger."

"Bullshit, don't say all of the things you think I want to hear, because if I didn't stop in that street after we made that pitiful bump of a connection, you would have continued on.

"You would have continued walking and rolled your eyes, and probably called me an asshole under your breath, but never to my face.

"Be honest. You would have never stopped to see the pain behind these glasses. People like me who are not just lost, but at a loss, are dying to feel love and life. We need something to breathe air back into our lungs because we have lost our purpose, we have forgotten why we are here, what all of this is even for and it hurts so bad. You don't understand how much it hurts inside. Humans are not built to feel this empty, and this—this is pointless. Do you know how many people stare at me because they can feel that I am hurting, but don't do anything?"

I could see the water forming in her eyes.

I let her finish talking.

"I'll be honest.

"If you didn't stop,
"I would have finished crossing that street.

"Waited for that light to turn green,
"walked back into the street
"and hoped that no one would stop."

All I could do was listen to this woman's duet
of a cry for help and her false assumptions of me.
Her expectations for me to answer confused me.
I wanted to save her, but I did not know what she
wanted. She made me so mad as she exercised my
patience. How could she assume so easily that I was
like everyone else?

I knew in that moment that Loss was at either
spectrum of extreme. She was not living in the
moment. She did not understand life, and that in order
to live she needed love; she needed to let herself feel
another human being again. She focused too much on
the past, which led to depression. It led her to be stuck
in limbo. Loss also focused too much on the future,
which caused her to be scared of losing love again and
terrified of how happy life could actually make her.
How life could breathe air back into her lungs on its
own. Loss didn't need another late-night sex brigade,
she didn't need another man to do it for her. So, her
anxiety grew. When Loss is happy, she is very, very
happy, but when Loss gets sad, she gets very, very sad
and when Loss gets very, very sad, she begins to think
that there are better things than living.

I would notice if Loss died.

Pocket Full of Poems III
<u>Loss.</u>

<u>Jigsaw</u>

"As dramatic of a spoken word piece this is, I wanted to challenge my readers' imagination. This spoken word piece is as much a written word piece. When reading Jigsaw, give your mind the chance to imagine: They were out of this world, yet the world wasn't ready for them. The world took the music of Michael Jackson, and Whitney Houston, and Amy Winehouse, and Ray Charles, and John Lennon, and so many more. But, once those artists showed that they were human, the world ripped them apart. At the end of the day, after giving so much of themselves ... what did they have left???
- Alyea Pierce

If You Want Art,
shovel through the treasures in his chest.
I vacuum-sucked his lips and placed his mouth in that box.

I Never want to hear my name in metaphor again.

His paintings were Complaints.
It's Selfish, I know.
So, I plucked each and every finger off and placed them in that Box.
Just to make him a tad bit more beautiful.

Different.
Like Maybe Glass could blow Art and maybe recreate
him.
Make him just a little more perfect.
Because Perfect is Never Perfect enough,
Perfection has never tasted human for long.

I threw his brain in that box too.

I thought, *he thought a little too outside of the box for
me.*

I never liked the lovely things.
Never appreciated the Art in how he took paper and
turned them into airplanes.
I preferred the art in ripping it apart,
peeling back the rings in his skin,
breaking him down,
taking,
taking,
taking,
until there is nothing left but mush,
goosh,
and mess.

So, he plugged his ears,
drew an "X" on his chest with my lipstick,
tasting of the empty in pavement.

And threw himself in that box.

I always loved the sweet melody of Michael Jackson,

but once he showed he was human
How easily we could rip him apart.

I always loved the sweet melody of Amy Whinehouse,
but once she showed she was human
How easily we could rip her apart.

I always loved the sweet melody of Ray Charles and
John Lennon and Whitney Houston and once they
showed that they were human
How easily we could rip them apart.

They threw themselves in that box.

Locked it and ate the key.

Clearly,
Only the Dead Live in Art.

The Giver

Peeling his skin open,

Ripping flesh,

digging her vein-throbbing,

blistered fingers

and heart-shaped palm into his left chest.

Then taking his palm-shaped heart and

throwing it on the ground.

The ground that makes eye contact easier to inhale.

The ground that leaks the words we do not speak.

Or, more of the three words that never get spit past our
tongues

                        And stomping on it.

He's lost.

It feels as if there's a slug in his lung.

Or, maybe all of the burning cigarettes he smoked to
calm his nerves ended up coating his breath with her.

He can't breathe.

She took his heart.

And from hers, he's been shunned.

We Wrapped this Gift

I threw your heart in a box and kept it for myself.
Is that selfish?

It hit the bottom loud,
like a firework cracking open the sky.

I enjoyed the echo.

It lasted longer than you ever did.

There was music in that box.

I threw every pair of broken, brown-soled loafers
we kicked around our hearts with, in that box.

We were proof that the word *young* doesn't hurt love,
but

                                        each other.

Fallen Autumn

Leaves don't crinkle the same way underneath my ton
of a body without you there.

Their veins don't resemble the lifelines in my palms
you traced between sheets.

They don't blow in the wind anymore.
                    They do nothing.

They are heavy and soggy,
                    They are grossly heavy.

Ugly, like New York city streets that only get to taste
the bottom of dirt-stained soles.

There is no more beautiful in this kind of ugly.

Heart Built of Bomb

I miss how New York's time ticks
over stained minds, wrestling with the idea of
motions, clocks slowly tock in. The empty
ticks stop roses and daffo-lions from tasting a new
flavor lithosphere. This is where
grandfather clocks chime me into a drunken daze;
the day silence strangled the twin towers, or
when Columbus sailed on a great whale and
discovered Jupiter.
Does truth speak in silence or in bombs?
Truth speaks in DaVinci,
                Angelo,
                Tesla and in blades of grass
when the wind howls.

But, we are still so late.

I am still so late because when I stood on that ledge,
Empire State high, and tasted
all of my last memories,
fireworks bled through the air screaming "Come
Home"
and I still did not know where I'd land with that next
step.

See You Later

I want to curse the air for its greed,
                       for taking his last breath.

My uncle had a body built of stories.
Stories that road-mapped themselves along the tender
of his skin,
        skin that hasn't felt grass walk on him since
cancer kissed his cells.

His stories have lived longer than him.

He told me once that he lives for the moments that
take his breath away.

So, if it weren't for cancer, he would have never
noticed the beauty in how my aunt still looked down,
like a fourth grader checking "yes" in love notes, when
he complimented her.

He would have never noticed her love,
                             how she was the
sun and he was the earth, and never once said,
"You Owe Me."

Or, how he had the chance to see, and feel, and inhale
such a woman.

I want to curse the air for its greed,
                       for taking his last breath.

But, how could I be so selfish?

My uncle thanked cancer.
                             For the tubes,
                             for the pain, for the aching pain,
                             for the prying and the picking,
        and   for the false hopes.

I miss him.

And I didn't say I loved him the last time we met, for I feared it would be the last time we'd meet.

But, I hear his laugh every time my cousins speak.
   See his smile in the concrete cracks in Bronx basketball courts.

His death shows me how much he has lived.

I had the chance to see, and feel, and inhale such a man.

                  I was the lucky one.

How to Speak to the Dead

First burn the striking sounds of reality with the candle
of living memories,
then turn the clock back 24 hours because heaven
works on a different time schedule.

Next, walk on to a green-lit field, drenched with the
colors of the rainbow.
Listen for the plucking violin strings, and
the slowly playing chamber orchestra strumming
behind the scenes.
But, you must be alone.
If, and only if you are alone and have properly
conducted the previous steps, you may proceed to the
next section: "The Dance of the Dead."

1st Go down low … How low can you go? … Go all
the way to the floor.
2nd Touch the ground in crouching position.
3rd One hop. (Yes, hop like a frog.)
4th Blink five times.
5th Close your eyes (squint as hard as you can!).
6th Put your hands in the air and *reach*.

Now, unfortunately the dead will not utter a word, or
the language you speak;
they have come to learn the dialect of the gods and
goddesses.
You must leave your hands in the air, and they will
touch you with their golden palms and you will feel
the words they say.

They will strip the earth of its faded soil and replenish the ground with meaning.
Each word you will feel through feeling will be as simple, and sweet, and elegant, and as alluring as the night sky.

Now, breathe.

Open your eyes.

The Party of Lost Children

We are the party of lost children.
The ones who have endless story growing from our heads.
We are the ones who are so quick to ride home when the streetlights come on, but we never go home to white picket fences, but to a place where welcome mats are flipped upside down,
Because we are the ones not welcome in our own home
Because no one will ever understand why we use excuses for water.
                              Why we use excuses for our art.
Home is any place far our minds can pedal to.
Where the night and us are on a first name basis, the north star rubs our backs, and the moon cradles our pupils.

We are the party of lost children.
We are the thinkers, the artists, the romantics, the dreamers, the crazy's,
Not the talkers.
We are the emo's, the goths, the bookworms, the nerds, the french fry turners who take pride in being not unoriginal.
We were not the cool kid in class,
but the back of our heads took it.
The back of our heads were the basket for every winning spit ball by the cool kid.
They needed us.

Like we need words.
Like we need silence.
Like we need to trap ourselves in our selves.

We are the party of lost children fighting to the death
with ourselves.
We are half dead, writing words that wrap around our
hearts like life vests because every time I say that this
is my last poem and wave it in the air like a white flag.
I said that this is my last poem and I am wearing it like
a white flag,
I remember how good it feels to be alone.
How good it feels to sit in the back of the class, bite
my nails and spit crucifixions at the cool kid.
I remember how good it feels to be the damn french
fry turner because I am damn good at it!

We are the party of lost children.
We are the glass half empty, not full.
Full is just too easy.

We may never be as great as the cool kid,
walk on Wall Street in a 3 piece suit,
we may be considered the little guy until the day we
die.
But, at least we have given a piece of ourselves every
day since we were born.

They needed us.

Part IV

Our DEEPEST Craving.

...is to be connected to another human being, not JUST a stranger, but a human turned friend. We die to feel; to be loved; to know that we matter.

Why Poetry?

Because in harsh ice storms metal can bend.

Without it, simple winds can break bright street lights,

Without it, scribbling outside the lines of Hail Marys will be easy,

And without it, gravity pulls down kites.

Why Poetry?

Because children can wish in wishing wells and everything *will* be OK,

And this love can smile like a skyline.

Poetry is you. It is me. Poetry is everything. It is everything and anything we want it to be.
- Alyea Pierce

If Poetry had a voice...
It would say that it changed my life.

It would say,

Play with your food.

Put your hand just a little bit closer to the fire.

Make a mess.

If Poetry had a voice it would say that

You

are a dreamer,

So, ask why, every time.

It would say,

Practice kissing the inside of your elbow because there is probably a part of you that is still insecure.

It would say that

I am more than *To Be's*, and *Not To Be's*,

Because I am NOT ONLY SHAKESPEARE and HAMLET!

Poetry would say that I am not about who has the greatest number of snaps, or literary journals published.

Because Poetry is about truth.

It is an opportunity,

one moment in time where nothing matters.

Where you can make an audience member, a reader,

feel, taste, smell, hear, see what you are saying.

You are the connector to making the intangible, tangible.

Giving breath to words by picking pecks of adverbs, and adjectives, and creating your own story.

Poets are story tellers.

I come from a West Indian background, in which my father is Jamaican and my mother is Trinidadian and Venezuelan, and in these cultures, being that my family has fought many barriers to come to America,

expressing emotions is sort of looked down upon and Poetry was my emotional outlet.

So in turn, Poetry will always be looked down upon in my family. It will never be real enough.

When I performed on the Apollo and Broadway stages, some of my family did not even want to come because to them, Poetry is complaining.

Except for my great-aunt.

She was a poet.

She loved crossword puzzles.

86

She loved a world where words didn't move together to create stories or lies,

but facts.

Without her …

I would have no voice.

You see, Poetry is scary. The root of Poetry is about being as raw as possible. It is supposed to be messy and uncomfortable and scary. But it is OK to be scared.

If Poetry had a voice, it would say,

I can help you feel as free as you felt when you ran around naked as a baby.

Poetry would say that I can transform your "I love yous" and "I miss yous" into real statements you can feel, not just overused phrases.

For example, instead of saying,

"I miss you,"

I am a hummingbird who has lost its voice.

Or instead of "I love you,"

Let me sing you the oldest-known love song that sits

on the river floor of Tigris and Euphrates.

So if this is poetry,

If this is what truth looks like, I'm sure you're asking, "What makes it valuable to me? Why is it valuable to me? What does this even have to do with me?"

Studies show that speaking aloud activates the brain.

Writing by hand activates the brain.

Your truth activates the brain.

Creativity,

honesty, and

voice are necessary to being human.

The telegraph states that "Putting pen to paper is said to help the brain regulate emotion."

Thinking creatively and writing by hand is the beginning to answering every question you have ever asked,

And expressing one's true emotions is therapeutic.

Writing about yourself through the exploration of your feelings makes you think about certain ignored emotions, which better helps you gain insight into your inner self.

I don't think we even realize how ignored our feelings are.

We are becoming products of a tighten-your-tie,

tuck-your-shirt-in,

and tie-your-shoelaces kind of world.

But I prefer tripping around.

It's a tad bit more fun.

If Poetry had a voice, it would say YOU are Poetry.

Even if you have never written a word or just called your mama today,

You have experienced poetry on some level.

But what humors me is that people think poetry has to be extravagant. Flamboyant. Big.

No.

A pickup line from the grandfather to the old woman in the nursing home he's had his eyes on is poetry.

A knock-knock joke from the little girl to her father on an afternoon bench is poetry.

Look at the person next to you.

I mean, really look.

Loooooooooooooook. (Thank You.)

If Poetry had a voice, you're feeling it right now.

Acknowledgments:

The only time I allow myself to bow my head is when I pray and when I humbly bow to say Thank You to those who continue to lift me through their creations.

-Alyea Pierce

Thank you to **Graphic Designer, Anthony Gibbons** (Booking Inquiries: Me@AntGibbz.com) for designing my book cover. Thank you to **Photographer, Ron Downes Jr.** (Booking Inquiries: ronronproductionz@gmail.com) for providing me with my headshot on the front cover. Lastly, but never least, Thank you to **Photographer, Andrew Forino** (Booking Inquiries: Afphotos@aol.com) for allowing me to use the strangers photos that make up my face on the front cover from his "Faces of Savannah" album. Each and every one of you are angels. Thank you so much for using your gifts to help my dream come true.

Family: To the World's Best family! We are a circus, but I love each and every one of you. You have taught me humor, love, respect, and what a blessing it is to listen. I could not write this book if I did not listen. Each and every one of you deserves so much more than a Thank You. Each of you is my heart and soul. I do not know where I would be without you. I have dreams that sound insane, but I believe so much in them...and each of you do too. Thank you for believing and not giving up on me.

The Gyals and Second Moms: Words can't express my appreciation for each and every one of you in my life. Your belief in me and support is truly unreal. I couldn't ask for better second families. All of you have helped shape the young woman I am today and I learn how to be a better woman because of each of you. Thank you.

Rutgers, New York and Somerset, NJ: All of these communities have become my second home. If it were not for the New Jersey Orators, Phi Delta Kappa, Epsilon Alpha Chapter Inc. Xinos, and ACT-SO New Brunswick fostering and nurturing my oratorical/ poetic gift, I would not stand here today. Thank you. As I traveled on to RU, Thank you to Rutgers Professor Vondell Richmond for helping me realize that if I do not follow my dreams, I would end up helping someone else achieve theirs. He created this 30 day Writers Academy. YES! I wrote this book in 30 Days!!! HE IS INSANE! But, Thank you for the challenge! Thank you to Rutgers Professors Evie Shockley, and Joshua Ballinger for teaching me the true definition of self- determination, perseverance, and tenacity. Sometimes you have to push yourself. Thank you!

Thank you to the RUTGERS COMMUNITY, all of the fraternities, sororities, verbal mayhem and student organizations who see the value in my art and assisted in my growth and my business' growth.

Thank you to Urban Word NYC! You are more than poets, you are game changers and a family that I can always come back to.

Who is *Alyea Pierce* and What Advice Does She Have for you?

Make your dreams so much of a reality that they become a lifestyle.

-Alyea Pierce

Alyea Pierce describes herself as a Chex Mix of the West Indian islands who is Walking Poetry. Alyea, a hopeFUL romantic, is a 20 year old senior attending Rutgers University New Brunswick. She was a finalist in the New York Knicks Poetry Slam, and the New York Teen Slams. She is a Poetry Mentor, Public Speaking coach, Workshop Instructor, and a member of the 2012 Rutgers Slam Team, who placed 11th in the nation at the College Unions Poetry Slam Invitational in California, and team leader of the 2013 team. Her work has been featured on platforms such as the Apollo Theater, Broadway's New Amsterdam Theater, Nuyorican Poet's Cafe, The Bowery, Columbia University, Kean University, TEDx Rutgers and more than 75 events at Rutgers University. Alyea Pierce has also taught high school students who have gone on to win state and regional oratorical/ poetry titles. She strives to be a world-traveled motivational speaker and poet, teaching children the beauty of art and voice through poetry.

I have been married since I was 11 years old. It has been one relationship, ongoing 10 years now. I know that sounds crazy, but Poetry has taken my heart. Being in the business of marketing products, programs and services for people to help them change their lives for the better through poetry and being a 20-year-old young woman, sometimes makes it very difficult to separate the two. It is often easier to write how I feel than to say it, and for many people that is hard to understand. Even though I have performed in front of thousands on some of the most prestigious stages, I am scared. I will always be the shy kid in class when it comes to my feelings. Every time I touch a stage, I am giving a part of my heart to an audience of strangers. Every time I walk up to a mic, I must breathe and say, "Everything will be OK," because it will.

It is an interesting moment when the page speaks louder than yourself. But in the past, I didn't even trust my pen. In the past, I would have to think, *Does this make sense? Will they like it?* Trusting that you have a right to say what you have to say is essential. These several different philosophies apply to the main theme of this book, *balance.* I know how being unbalanced can really turn a world upside down. Balance is key and I tight-roped along a thin line with portraying balance, conveying the ugly and beautiful that I see in this world and in myself through this book.

Thank you for appreciating my honesty and truth. Strangers want to hear something real, they want to feel connected by their hearts, and know that they are not alone. I want to know that I am not alone and a community of writers helps to provide that. From now on, I want to be part of your community. **Join the Journey!** We all want to make our writing the best it can be and, to that end, we all need advice from time to time. One thing I will say is never underestimate what you consider to be "bad" writing. Ever. Every word you think, every word you have written, has a purpose. Every part of you and from you is good and worthy of being labeled "good writing", but, don't write to please anybody or anything. Please. It took me too long to learn that. Even if you just write a page of *blah blah blahs*, or *I just don't know what to do anymore's*, those things are important. Write to free yourself, not to trap yourself. It took me awhile to realize that I was writing for other people, and when I wrote my first honest piece, it literally looked like a diary entry. Something as simple as that made me cry like a baby.

Sit in the dark. Sit in front of a mirror. Shut the door. Be by yourself. Breathe. Close your eyes and write; don't look at the page. Write the first things that come to your mind and DON'T ERASE! Those first few things mean something to you. They are the answer to some dying question you have.

In your truth, you will find beauty, and in such beauty, you will find yourself, my dear.

Thank You.

The *Every Stranger* **Program Package:**

<u>The Write to Slam Workshop:</u>

Contact <u>AlyeaSPierce@gmail.com</u> to bring this program to YOU!

For the launch of my book I am discounting this 90 minute workshop starting at $250.00!

Alyea Pierce transforms your school, right on cite into a real live poetry slam environment that will:

1. be specifically tailored to grades 6-12 or college students.

2. help 6-12 grade teachers incorporate aspects of the youth slam poetry movement into their English curriculum.

3. transform what students go through daily into a creative form of expression and teach students how to confidently and productively use their voice.

If you would like a <u>Custom-Made</u> Workshop

tailored to your High School, University, or Community organization contact <u>Alyeaspierce@gmail.com</u> for a consultation!

Take a picture of you with the *Every Stranger Deserves a Poem* book, tag AlyeaSpeaks and post it on Instagram, Twitter, or Facebook!

YOUR TAG= A DISCOUNT to the very FIRST

Write to Speak Open Mic!

Tell Alyea what YOUR Favorite Poem was on Instagram, Facebook, or Twitter and don't forget to send your very own original pieces to the

Every Stranger Journey! YouTube channel!

To get involved in the 30 Day Writer's Academy which assisted in my completion of this book

Contact:Vondellcoaches@gmail.com

and write *Alyea Pierce Writer's Academy* in the subject section.

Website: TheWriteToSpeak.com

YouTube: To Follow Alyea's personal work AlyeaPiercePoetry

Tumblr: AlyeaPierce

The Every Stranger Journey!

_____

_____

_____

_____

_____

_____

_____

_____

_____

_____

_____

_____

_____

_____

Made in the USA
San Bernardino, CA
22 August 2014